Ke

by Iain Gray

Lang**Syne**
PUBLISHING
WRITING *to* REMEMBER

Lang**Syne**

PUBLISHING

WRITING *to* REMEMBER

E-mail: info@lang-syne.co.uk

Distributed in the Republic of Ireland by Portfolio Group,
Kilbarrack Ind. Est. Kilbarrack, Dublin 5.
T:00353(01) 839 4918 F:00353(01) 839 5826
sales@portfoliogroup.ie
www.portfoliogroup.ie

Design by Dorothy Meikle   Printed by Ricoh Print Scotland

© Lang Syne Publishers Ltd 2013

All rights reserved. No part of this publication may be reproduced, stored
or introduced into a retrieval system, or transmitted in any form or by any
means (electronic, mechanical, photocopying, recording or otherwise) without
the prior written permission of Lang Syne Publishers Ltd.

ISBN 978-1-85217-570-2

Kennedy

MOTTO:
Cling to virtue
(and)
The uppermost hand.

CREST:
An arm, embowed, with
the hand grasping a scimitar.

NAME variations include:
Kennedie
O' Kennedy
Ó Cinnéide *(Gaelic)*
Ó Ceannéidigh *(Gaelic)*

Chapter one:
Origins of Irish surnames

According to an old saying, there are two types of Irish – those who actually are Irish and those who wish they were.

This sentiment is only one example of the allure that the high romance and drama of the proud nation's history holds for thousands of people scattered across the world today.

It's a sad fact, however, that the vast majority of Irish surnames are found far beyond Irish shores, rather than on the Emerald Isle itself.

The population stood at around eight million souls in 1841, but today it stands at fewer than six million.

This is mainly a tragic consequence of the potato famine, also known as the Great Hunger, which devastated Ireland between 1845 and 1849.

The Irish peasantry had become almost wholly reliant for basic sustenance on the potato, first introduced from the Americas in the seventeenth century.

When the crop was hit by a blight, at least 800,000 people starved to death while an estimated two million others were forced to seek a new life far from their native shores – particularly in America, Canada, and Australia.

The effects of the potato blight continued until about 1851, by which time a firm pattern of emigration had become established.

Ireland's loss, however, was to the gain of the countries in which the immigrants settled, contributing enormously, as their descendants do today, to the well being of the nations in which their forefathers settled.

But those who were forced through dire circumstance to establish a new life in foreign parts never forgot their roots, or the proud heritage and traditions of the land that gave them birth.

Nor do their descendants.

It is a heritage that is inextricably bound up in the colourful variety of Irish names themselves – and the origin and history of these names forms an integral part of the vibrant drama that is the nation's history, one of both glorious fortune and tragic misfortune.

This history is well documented, and one of the most important and fascinating of the earliest sources are *The Annals of the Four Masters*, compiled between 1632 and 1636 by four friars at the Franciscan Monastery in County Donegal.

Compiled from earlier sources, and purporting to go back to the Biblical Deluge, much of the material takes in the mythological origins and history of Ireland and the Irish.

This includes tales of successive waves of invaders and settlers such as the Fomorians, the Partholonians, the Nemedians, the Fir Bolgs, the Tuatha De Danann, and the Laigain.

Of particular interest are the *Milesian Genealogies*,

because the majority of Irish clans today claim a descent from either Heremon, Ir, or Heber – three of the sons of Milesius, a king of what is now modern day Spain.

These sons invaded Ireland in the second millennium B.C, apparently in fulfilment of a mysterious prophecy received by their father.

This Milesian lineage is said to have ruled Ireland for nearly 3,000 years, until the island came under the sway of England's King Henry II in 1171 following what is known as the Cambro-Norman invasion.

This is an important date not only in Irish history in general, but for the effect the invasion subsequently had for Irish surnames.

'Cambro' comes from the Welsh, and 'Cambro-Norman' describes those Welsh knights of Norman origin who invaded Ireland.

But they were invaders who stayed, inter-marrying with the native Irish population and founding their own proud dynasties that bore Cambro-Norman names such as Archer, Barbour, Brannagh, Fitzgerald, Fitzgibbon, Fleming, Joyce, Plunkett, and Walsh – to name only a few.

These 'Cambro-Norman' surnames that still flourish throughout the world today form one of the three main categories in which Irish names can be placed – those of Gaelic-Irish, Cambro-Norman, and Anglo-Irish.

Previous to the Cambro-Norman invasion of the twelfth century, and throughout the earlier invasions and settlement of those wild bands of sea rovers known as the Vikings in the eighth and ninth centuries, the population of the island was relatively small, and it was normal for a person to be identified through the use of only a forename.

But as population gradually increased and there were many more people with the same forename, surnames were adopted to distinguish one person, or one community, from another.

Individuals identified themselves with their own particular tribe, or 'tuath', and this tribe – that also became known as a clann, or clan – took its name from some distinguished ancestor who had founded the clan.

The Gaelic-Irish form of the name Kelly, for example, is Ó Ceallaigh, or O'Kelly, indicating descent from an original 'Ceallaigh', with the 'O' denoting 'grandson of.' The name was later anglicised to Kelly.

The prefix 'Mac' or 'Mc', meanwhile, as with the clans of the Scottish Highlands, denotes 'son of.'

Although the Irish clans had much in common with their Scottish counterparts, one important difference lies in what are known as 'septs', or branches, of the clan.

Septs of Scottish clans were groups who often bore an entirely different name from the clan name but were under the clan's protection.

In Ireland, septs were groups that shared the same name and who could be found scattered throughout the four provinces of Ulster, Leinster, Munster, and Connacht.

The 'golden age' of the Gaelic-Irish clans, infused as their veins were with the blood of Celts, pre-dates the Viking invasions of the eighth and ninth centuries and the Norman invasion of the twelfth century, and the sacred heart of the country was the Hill of Tara, near the River Boyne, in County Meath.

Known in Gaelic as 'Teamhar na Rí', or Hill of Kings, it was the royal seat of the 'Ard Rí Éireann', or High King of Ireland, to whom the petty kings, or chieftains, from the island's provinces were ultimately subordinate.

It was on the Hill of Tara, beside a stone pillar known as the Irish 'Lia Fáil', or Stone of Destiny, that the High Kings were inaugurated and, according to legend, this stone would emit a piercing screech that could be heard all over Ireland when touched by the hand of the rightful king.

The Hill of Tara is today one of the island's main tourist attractions.

Opposition to English rule over Ireland, established in the wake of the Cambro-Norman invasion, broke out frequently and the harsh solution adopted by the powerful forces of the Crown was to forcibly evict the native Irish from their lands.

These lands were then granted to Protestant colonists, or 'planters', from Britain.

Many of these colonists, ironically, came from Scotland and were the descendants of the original 'Scotti', or 'Scots', who gave their name to Scotland after migrating there in the fifth century A.D., from the north of Ireland.

Colonisation entailed harsh penal laws being imposed on the majority of the native Irish population, stripping them practically of all of their rights.

The Crown's main bastion in Ireland was Dublin and its environs, known as the Pale, and it was the dispossessed peasantry who lived outside this Pale, desperately striving to eke out a meagre living.

It was this that gave rise to the modern-day expression of someone or something being 'beyond the pale'.

Attempts were made to stamp out all aspects of the ancient Gaelic-Irish culture, to the extent that even to bear a Gaelic-Irish name was to invite discrimination.

This is why many Gaelic-Irish names were anglicised with, for example, and noted above, Ó Ceallaigh, or O'Kelly, being anglicised to Kelly.

Succeeding centuries have seen strong revivals of Gaelic-Irish consciousness, however, and this has led to many families reverting back to the original form of their name, while the language itself is frequently found on the fluent tongues of an estimated 90,000 to 145,000 of the island's population.

Ireland's turbulent history of religious and political strife is one that lasted well into the twentieth century, a landmark century that saw the partition of the island into the twenty-six counties of the independent Republic of

Ireland, or Eire, and the six counties of Northern Ireland, or Ulster.

Dublin, originally founded by Vikings, is now a vibrant and truly cosmopolitan city while the proud city of Belfast is one of the jewels in the crown of Ulster.

It was Saint Patrick who first brought the light of Christianity to Ireland in the fifth century A.D.

Interpretations of this Christian message have varied over the centuries, often leading to bitter sectarian conflict – but the many intricately sculpted Celtic Crosses found all over the island are symbolic of a unity that crosses the sectarian divide.

It is an image that fuses the 'old gods' of the Celts with Christianity.

All the signs from the early years of this new millennium indicate that sectarian strife may soon become a thing of the past – with the Irish and their many kinsfolk across the world, be they Protestant or Catholic, finding common purpose in the rich tapestry of their shared heritage.

Chapter two:
On the field of battle

A name of truly ancient pedigree rooted deep in the soil of the Emerald Isle, 'Kennedy' has two possible points of origin.

In common with many other surnames, it derives from what was originally a forename – while Irish-Gaelic forms of this given name are Cinnéide and Ceannéidigh.

The surname Ó Cinnéide denotes 'grandson of Cinnéide', while Ó Ceannéidigh denotes 'grandson of Ceannéidigh.'

'Ceannéidigh', meanwhile, derives from *ceann*, indicating 'head' or 'leader', while *éidigh* indicates 'ugly' or 'grim' – and both Ceannéidigh and Cinnéide may originally have denoted 'grim-headed' or even 'helmet-headed.'

Intriguingly, the ancient Coat of Arms of the Ó Cinnéides, or Kennedys, features three helmets in profile, helmets that would have been worn in battle.

This indicates that the appellation of 'grim- headed' or 'helmet-headed' may therefore have originally been descriptive of a warrior chief, clad for combat, the very sight of whom on the bloody field of battle would have struck terror into the hearts of his enemies.

Also, in keeping with the martial tradition of the

Kennedys, the Crest of their Coat of Arms features an embowed arm with the hand firmly grasping a scimitar.

Travelling back through the dim mists of time, 'Ceannéidigh' is also thought to relate to the Gaelic name 'Cénnetig', and further unravelling a highly complex genealogical skene, this is why some bearers of the Kennedy name today may trace a descent from some of Ireland's most colourful and illustrious historical figures.

Foremost among them is Brian Boru, or Brian Boruma, also known as Brian mac Cennétig, son of Cennétig MacLorcain, a tenth century king of the territory known as Thomond, in the province of Munster, and which embraced most of the modern day counties of Tipperary, Limerick, Clare and Kerry.

In common with the more dominant O'Briens, Boru's lineage was of the mighty tribal grouping known as the DálgCais, the Race of Cas, or Dalcassians, and whose territory was Dal Cas in the upper reaches of Thomond.

This powerful grouping was named from the legendary Cormac Cas, the early to mid-third century chieftain of Munster who was renowned for his remarkable, courage, strength and dexterity.

He inflicted a celebrated defeat on the men of the province of Leinster in a battle fought near present day Wexford, but was killed in battle in 254 A.D. at Dun-tri-Lag, or the Fort of the Stone Slabs, known today as Duntrileague, in Co. Limerick.

His deathblow, according to the ancient annals, came from the spear of the Leinster king known rather colourfully as Eochy of the Red Eyebrows.

It is from a descendant of Cormac Cas that the proud O'Briens take their name, while it was the Dalcassian Brian Boru, ancestor of the Kennedys, who stamped an indelible mark on Ireland's historical record.

This was at the battle of Clontarf, fought about four miles north of Dublin on Good Friday of 1014.

Late tenth and early eleventh century Ireland was the scene of vicious inter-clan rivalry as successive chiefs fought for supremacy over their rivals.

It was this disunity that worked to the advantage of the Norman invaders of the twelfth century and the Viking invaders of previous centuries.

The period 795 A.D. to 1014 A.D. is known to Irish history as the Viking Tyranny, and it was largely through the inspired leadership of Brian Boru that Viking power was diminished, although not completely eliminated.

He was able to achieve this by managing to rally a number of chieftains to his cause – although by no means all.

With his battle-hardened warriors known as the Dalcassian knights at his side, Boru had by 1002 A.D. achieved the prize of Ard Rí Éireann, High King of Ireland, but there were still rival chieftains, and not least the Vikings, to contend with.

These Vikings, known as Ostmen, had occupied and fortified Dublin in the mid-ninth century and had other important trading settlements on other parts of the island.

Resenting Boru's High Kingship, a number of chieftains, particularly those of Leinster, found common cause with the Ostmen and the two sides met in final and bloody confrontation at Clontarf.

Boru proved victorious, but the annals speak of great slaughter on the day, with the dead, including the High King's three sons Murrough, Conaing and Moltha, piled high on the field of battle.

Boru had little time to celebrate his victory – being killed in his tent by a party of fleeing Vikings led by Brodar the Dane.

The first to enter the tent had his legs cut off with a sweep of the High King's mighty two-handed sword.

Brodar then struck him a fatal blow on the back of his head with his axe, but Boru rallied the last of his dying strength to cut of his assailant's head with another sweep of his sword before killing yet another Viking.

Brian Boru and all who had fought for him at Clontarf passed into legend, and the great warrior king was interred in a stone coffin on the north side of the high altar in Armagh Church.

It is through a nephew of Brian Boru, Mahon, son of Boru's older brother Donncuan, that the Kennedys trace a descent from the victor of the battle of Clontarf.

Mahon was the first to designate himself 'Ó Cinnéide', and the Ó Cinnéides, or Kennedys, came to hold sway in the region known as Ormond – comprising northern Tipperary, Mayo, northern Limerick and eastern Clare.

Before establishing themselves beyond the river Shannon in Ormond, they had been settled in Glenmor, near Killaloe.

The *Annals of the Four Masters* state that by 1300 the Kennedys were "undisputed Lords of Ormond", with castles that included Ballintotty, Dromineer, Garrykennedy and Nenagh – while the Kennedy name also survives on the Irish landscape to this day with place names that include Coolkennedy and Killokennedy.

So numerous were the Kennedys that they split into three branches, originally ruled over by chiefs who were distinguished from one another by their hair colour. Thus arose the *rua* (red) Kennedys, the *don* (brown) and the *fionn* (blond).

Adding complexity to the presence of bearers of the Kennedy name throughout the Emerald Isle today is that in the early years of the seventeenth century a number re-located north to settle in Co. Antrim, one of the six present day counties of Ulster, or Northern Ireland.

Meanwhile, there was also an influx of another totally separate group of Kennedys to Ulster.

These Kennedys, from the south-western Scottish coast of Galloway and the western coast of Ayrshire – all within relatively short sailing distance of the north of Ireland – were related to the Scottish Clan Kennedy, whose motto is *Consider the End* and crest a dolphin.

The proud Clan Kennedy, who supported the great Scottish warrior king Robert the Bruce during the Wars of Independence against England, achieved high honours and distinction with, in 1457, Gilbert Kennedy being created Lord Kennedy.

The seat of Clan Kennedy is Cassillis House, near Maybole, in Ayrshire, while their former seat was the magnificent Culzean Castle, which remains a major tourist attraction to this day.

Other properties include Dunure Castle and Greenan Castle, while the Chief of the Name of Kennedy is The Most Honourable Archibald Angus Charles Kennedy, 8th Marquess of Ailsa and Earl of Cassillis.

Those Kennedys who settled in Ulster from Scotland did so through what was known as the policy of 'plantation', the settlement of loyal Protestants on lands held by native Irish that was started during the reign from 1491 to 1547 of Henry VIII, and whose Reformation effectively outlawed the Roman Catholic faith throughout his dominions.

The plantation continued throughout the subsequent reigns of Elizabeth I, James I (James VI of Scotland) and in the wake of the Cromwellian invasion of 1649.

It was during the reign of James I that many 'Scottish'

Kennedys were settled in Ulster – where their descendants remain to this day as part of a proud Ulster-Scots heritage.

It is because of the intermingling of original native Irish Ó Cinnéides, or Kennedys, and those whose roots are in Scotland, that *all* Kennedys on the Emerald Isle today are recognised by the Chief of the Scottish Clan Kennedy as part of the clan and therefore entitled to share in its honours and traditions.

Chapter three:
Wealth and power

It was in June of 1963 that U.S. President John Fitzgerald "Jack" Kennedy, also known as JFK, paid a four-day state visit to the Irish Republic.

In many ways it was a homecoming for the charismatic 35th President of the United States, for it was from Ireland that his paternal great-grandfather had emigrated in the early years of the nineteenth century for a new life in America – and, unwittingly, laying the foundations for one of the nation's greatest and wealthiest political dynasties.

In addition to becoming the first foreign leader to address the Houses of the Oireachtas, the Irish Parliament, President Kennedy also visited the humble cottage at Dunganstown, near the town of New Ross, in Co. Wexford, where his great-grandfather Patrick Kennedy had been born in about 1823 – a descendant of the original native Irish Ó Cinnéides.

The son of a farmer and one of three children, it was his older brother who inherited the family farm following the death of their parents.

At the time of the Irish potato famine and with scant prospect of being able to maintain a living in his native land, Patrick Kennedy departed for America when he was aged 26.

He had already been taught the skills of coopering, or barrel making, by a friend who worked in a brewery in New Ross.

This friend, Patrick Barron, had left for America before Kennedy and he welcomed him when he arrived in Boston.

Obtaining employment as a cooper, he later married Bridget Murphy, a cousin of Barron, and the couple had five children who included Patrick Joseph "P.J." Kennedy, also known as Joe Kennedy.

Patrick Kennedy died of cholera shortly after P.J.'s birth in 1858, and his widow Bridget went on to establish a highly successful grocery and liquor store in Boston.

Educated at both Boston Latin School and Harvard University, the ambitious Joe Kennedy entered the world of finance and, through shrewd stock market investments and investment in a range of enterprises that included real estate, the steel industry and even the Hollywood movie industry, soon accrued a substantial fortune.

Also appointed to political office, the Democrat Joe Kennedy served from 1936 to 1938 as 1st Chairman of the U.S. Maritime Commission, 1st Chairman of the Securities and Exchange Commission and, from 1938 to late 1940, as U.S. Ambassador to the United Kingdom.

It was while in the latter post that he was effectively consigned to the political wilderness after declaring, in war-torn Britain, that "democracy is finished."

In 1914, Joe Kennedy had married Rose Elizabeth

Fitzgerald, eldest daughter of his political rival at the time John Francis "Honey Fitz" Fitzgerald.

The couple had nine children between 1915 and 1932, but it was a family afflicted with tragedy, leading to what was referred to as "the Kennedy curse."

Their oldest son, Joe Kennedy, Jr., was killed at the age of 29 in an aeroplane crash over the English Channel in 1944 while serving as a U.S. Navy pilot.

A daughter, Rose Marie "Rosemary" Kennedy, born in 1918, underwent a lobotomy in 1941 which left her severely incapacitated; institutionalised in 1949, she died in 2005.

Following the death of Joe Kennedy, Jr., Joe Kennedy Sr. invested his hopes for Kennedy family political greatness in the person of his second son John Fitzgerald Kennedy, born in 1917.

Working carefully behind the scenes and utilising his financial and political clout, Joe Kennedy was able to steer his son towards a career in politics.

This included, following a distinguished Second World War naval career, election as a Democrat to the House of Representatives in 1947, election to the U.S. Senate and, the greatest prize of all, election in 1961 as President of the United States.

As 35th President, he was the youngest to hold the powerful office while he was the first and, to date, the only Catholic to hold the office.

His powerful cabinet or 'court' of appointees and advisors, known as 'Camelot', signalled a Golden Age in American politics.

Key events during his tenure in office included the African-American Civil Rights Movement and his support for landmark legislation to improve the lot of African-Americans, the abortive Bay of Pigs invasion of Cuba, the Space Race with the Soviet Union, the building of the Berlin Wall and the very early stages of the Vietnam War.

But the Golden Age of Camelot came to a tragic end on Friday, November 22, 1963, when he was assassinated while on a visit to Dallas, Texas.

Travelling in a motorcade through the city with his wife, Jacqueline, beside him, he was shot three times; rushed to Parklands Hospital, he was pronounced dead shortly afterwards.

Lee Harvey Oswald, an employee of the Texas School Book Depository from where the fatal shots were believed to have been fired, was taken into police custody.

Claiming that he had been a 'patsy' in the affair – set up to take all the blame – he was shot and killed two days after the assassination by the nightclub owner Jack Ruby while being taken from custody in a Dallas police station.

An investigation into the Kennedy assassination, the Warren Commission, concluded that Oswald had been a lone assassin – but a much later United States House Select Committee on Assassinations, after carefully re-examining all the evidence, determined that JFK had 'probably' been assassinated as part of a much wider and carefully organised conspiracy.

Further tragedy struck the Kennedy family in 1968 when JFK's brother, Robert Francis Kennedy, better known as Bobby Kennedy, was assassinated at the age of 43.

Having been appointed by his brother as U.S. Attorney General, it was while campaigning for the Democratic presidential nomination that he was shot and killed by a 24-year-old Palestinian, Sirhan Sirhan, after addressing supporters in the Ambassador Hotel, Los Angeles.

His younger brother, Edward Moore "Ted" Kennedy, born in 1932, meanwhile served as Senator for Massachusetts for close on 47 years; he died in 2009. His son Patrick J. Kennedy is a U.S. Congressman.

Joe Kennedy, Sr. died in 1969, while his wife Rose died in 1995 at the age of 104.

Their daughter Kathleen Agnes "Kick" Kennedy, born in 1920 and who became Marchioness of Huntington following her marriage to William "Billy" Cavendish, was killed in an aircraft crash in France in 1948.

Her sister Eunice Mary Kennedy, born in 1921 and who died in 2009, was an international advocate for the disabled and the founder of the Special Olympics. Her younger sister, Jean Ann Kennedy, born in 1928, served from 1993 to 1998 as U.S. Ambassador to Ireland.

It had been in 1953 that the future President Kennedy

had married Jacqueline "Jackie" Lee Bouvier. Five years after her husband's assassination she married the Greek shipping tycoon Aristotle Onassis, who died in 1975; after pursuing a career in the arts, including as a book editor, she died in 1994.

She and JFK were the parents of four children – one child was born stillborn in 1956 – while Patrick Bouvier Kennedy died from infant respiratory disease only two days after his birth in 1963.

Their son John Fitzgerald "John-John" Kennedy, the lawyer and magazine publisher born in 1960, was killed in an aeroplane crash along with his wife and her sister in 1999.

His sister, Caroline Bouvier Kennedy, born in 1957, is the president of the John F. Kennedy Library Association, while her sister Maria Owings Shriver, born in 1955, is the journalist and author who was married for a time to the actor and Republican California Governor Arnold Schwarzenegger.

Among the many memorials throughout the world today to the late President Kennedy is a statue of him unveiled by his sister Jean at New Ross, Co. Wexford, in 2008.

There is also the magnificent John F. Kennedy Arboretum near New Ross and the J.F. Kennedy Memorial Park in Eyre Square, Co. Galway.

Still in the Kennedy homeland of Ireland and in the

world of politics, Hugh Kennedy, born in Dublin in 1879, was one of the architects of the Constitution of the Irish Free State, which was established in December of 1922.

Appointed the first Attorney General of the Irish Free State and later its first Chief Justice, he died in 1936.

In contemporary politics, Charles Kennedy, born in Inverness in 1959, is the British Liberal Democrat politician who led the party from August of 1999 until January of 2006.

Member of Parliament (MP) for the Scottish constituency of Ross, Skye and Lochaber, he was elected rector of Glasgow University in 2008 and then again in 2011.

Born in Glasgow in 1950, Helena Ann Kennedy, elevated to the Peerage of the United Kingdom in 1997 as Lady Kennedy of The Shaws, in Cathcart, Glasgow, is the leading barrister, broadcaster and Labour member of the House of Lords whose father, Joshua Kennedy, was a printer with the Scottish newspaper the *Daily Record* and a trade's union official.

The recipient of a number of honours and awards, she is also a former chair of the Human Genetics Commission.

Knighted in 1994 for his services to journalism, Ludovic Kennedy was the journalist, author and broadcaster born in Edinburgh in 1919.

An investigative reporter, he exposed a number of miscarriages of justice that include the wrongful conviction and hanging of Timothy Evans for crimes actually committed by his landlord John Christie.

This is detailed in Kennedy's 1961 book *Ten Rillington Place*, adapted for a film of the same name in 1970.

Married to the actress Moira Shearer, he died three years after her death in 2006.

Chapter four:
On the world stage

The recipient of a star on the Hollywood Walk of Fame, George Harris Kennedy, Jr. is the veteran American actor of film and television better known as George Kennedy.

Born into a show business family in New York City in 1925 – his father an orchestra leader and his mother a dancer – he made his stage debut at the tender age of only two.

Serving in the United States Army during the Second World War after having embarked on a career as a radio performer, he worked for U.S. Armed Forces Radio and was closely involved in the setting up of the U.S. Army Information Service.

Returning to the entertainment industry at the end of the conflict, he became a technical adviser for the popular *Sergeant Bilko* television series, while his first major film role came in the 1961 *The Little Shepherd of Kingdom Come*.

Further film credits include the 1963 *Charade*, the 1964 *Hush...Hush Sweet Charlotte*, the 1967 *Cool Hand Luke* – for which he won an Academy Award for Best Supporting Actor – the 1975 disaster movie *Airport* and the *Naked Gun* series of comedy films.

Other film credits include *The Dirty Dozen*, *Thunderbolt*

and Lightfoot, *The Eiger Sanction* and *Death on the Nile*, while television credits include the role of Carter McKay from 1988 to 1991 in *Dallas*.

Starring beside other early comedy greats such as Laurel and Hardy and the Marx Brothers and one of the original Keystone Cops, **Edgar Kennedy** was the American film actor born in 1890 in Monterey County, California and who died in 1948.

A heavyweight boxer before taking to the stage, his many film credits include the Marx Brothers 1933 classic *Duck Soup*, the 1937 *A Star is Born* and, from 1949 released a year after his death, *My Dream Is Yours*.

Discovered by James Cagney and starring beside him as his younger brother in the 1940 film *City of Conquest*, **Arthur Kennedy** was the American actor of stage and film born in 1914 in Worcester, Massachusetts.

Other film credits include the 1957 *Peyton Place*, the 1958 *Some Come Running* – for which he was nominated for an Academy Award for Best Supporting Actor – the 1968 *Anzio* and, from 1989, *Champion*.

Also the winner of a Tony Award for Best Supporting Actor in a production of Arthur Miller's *Death of a Salesman*, he died in 1990.

Bearers of the Kennedy name have also excelled in the highly competitive world of sport.

In the rough and tumble that is the fast-paced game of Irish hurling, **Jimmy Kennedy**, born in 1890 in

Carrigtwohill, Co. Kerry, and known in Gaelic as Séamus Ó Cinnéide, was the famed full-forward who played for the Cork senior team between 1912 and 1927.

Nicknamed "Major", his local club was Carrigtwohill, while he was the recipient of one Cork title, one All Ireland title and four Munster titles.

On the fields of European football, **Alan Kennedy**, born in Sunderland in 1954, is the English former left back who, in addition to earning two caps playing for his national team in 1984, played for clubs over a period of 22 years that include Newcastle United, Liverpool, Belgian club Beerschot and, from 1993 to 1994, Barrow.

He is an uncle of the football defender **Tom Kennedy**, born in Bury in 1985 and who has played for teams that include Bury, Rochdale, Leicester City and, from 2012, Barnsley.

Born in 1983 in Bellshill, North Lanarkshire, **John Kennedy** is the Scottish retired centre back who played for Celtic from 1999 to 2009.

It was while making his debut with the Scottish national team in 2009 that he suffered a serious knee injury that forced his retirement from playing; he now works as a scout for Celtic.

From football to athletics, **Bob Kennedy**, born in 1970 in Westerville, Ohio, is recognised as one of America's greatest ever distance runners.

Nicknamed "Blazin' Bob" and the 1987 U.S. junior

champion in cross country, in 1996 he held the U.S. records for the 3000-metres and 5000-metres events.

Bearers of the Kennedy name have also excelled, and continue to excel, in the creative world of music.

The winner of two prestigious Ivor Novello Awards for his contribution to music and an inductee of the Songwriters Hall of Fame, **Jimmy Kennedy** was the prolific Irish songwriter born in 1902 in Clough, Co. Tyrone.

A civil servant for a time with the Colonial Office, he later embarked on a career as a songwriter – mainly as a lyricist – and composed and co-composed a number of popular classics.

These include the 1931 *Barmaids Song*, sung by Gracie Fields, the 1935 *Red Sails in the Sunset* and other memorable compositions such as *My Prayer*, *Teddy Bears' Picnic*, *Hokey Cokey*, *Harbour Lights* and *Isle of Capri*.

During the Second World War, serving as a captain in the Royal Artillery, he wrote the popular wartime song *We're Going to Hang out the Washing on the Siegfried Line*.

He died in 1984, a year after being awarded the CBE for his services to music.

A virtuoso of both the violin and the viola, **Nigel Kennedy** is the classically trained musician born into a gifted musical family in Brighton in 1956.

His grandfather, Lauri Kennedy, was a principal cellist with the BBC Symphony Orchestra, his grandmother Dorothy Kennedy a pianist, his father the principal cellist with the Royal Philharmonic Orchestra and his mother Scylla a pianist.

A child prodigy, it was after being trained at the Yehudi Menuhin School of Music and the Julliard School in New York that he made his recording debut in 1984 with Elgar's *Violin Concerto*.

He is recognised as having been responsible for popularising many classical pieces – his 1989 recording of Vivaldi's *The Four Seasons*, with the English Chamber Orchestra, one of the best-selling classical albums ever.

The recipient in 1997 of a BRIT Award for Outstanding Contribution to Classical Music and the 2001 Male Artist of the Year Award, he has also recorded classical renditions of the music of bands and artistes ranging from The Who and The Doors to Jimi Hendrix.

On Irish shores, **Brian Kennedy**, born in Belfast in 1966, is the singer and songwriter who competed for Ireland in the 2006 Eurovision Song Contest with his own composition *Every Song is a Cry for Love*, finishing in tenth place.

A backing singer on a number of Van Morrison recordings that include *Days Like This*, *Back on Top* and *A Night in San Francisco*, his solo albums include the 2000 *Won't You Take Me Home* and the 2008 *Interpretations*.

He is the younger brother of the singer and songwriter Martin Kennedy, better known as **Bap Kennedy**, born in Belfast in 1962.

With hit compositions that include *Moonlight Kiss*, featured in the 2001 romantic comedy film *Serendipity*, he also enjoyed success with the band Energy Orchard with albums that include the 1992 *Stop the Machine* and, from 1996, *Orchardville*.

On Scottish shores, Malcolm Martin Kennedy was the singer better known as **Calum Kennedy**, born on the Isle of Lewis in 1928 and who died in 2006.

A highly accomplished singer in both Gaelic and English, his recordings include the best-selling album *Islands of Scotland*, featuring the song *Land o' Heart's Desire*.

Married to the singer Anne Gillies, who died in 1974, he was the father of the singer, actress and broadcaster **Fiona Kennedy** who, in turn, is the mother of the Scottish actress **Sophie Kennedy-Clark**.

Bearers of the proud name of Kennedy have also gained fame and distinction through military service.

Born in 1947 in Frankfurt, Germany, **Claudia Kennedy** is the retired United States Army lieutenant general who in 1997 became the first female to reach the rank of three-star general.

Commissioned a second lieutenant in 1969 and a specialist in intelligence and cryptology, following her promotion to three-star general she was appointed Army Deputy Chief of Staff for Intelligence.

A member of the Military Intelligence Hall of Fame, she retired from military service in 2000.